PRAISE FOR MY THERAPIST TOLD ME TO WRITE THIS

"... a beautiful collection of thoughts, emotions and intentions coming from a vulnerable space."

I was deeply moved by the words and artistry of this book. I also felt immensely proud of the author even though we don't know each other! It is truly a beautiful collection of thoughts, emotions and intentions coming from a vulnerable space. I believe vulnerability can have a powerful and equally cathartic impact.

As a woman, I connected deeply with these words. I felt seen with a sense of comradery, and as a mother, I simply felt ... it all! Each poem felt like a love letter to all women, young and old. My first thought was of all of the women that I want to share this chapbook with.

KATIE MULLANEY, LCAT, ATR
(CREATIVE ARTS THERAPIST AT CREATE SPACE BUFFALO)

"... raw and unapologetic ..."

My Therapist Told Me to Write This: Poems for Our Daughters is a powerful collection of poems written by Jenna Schifferle. The book, as the title suggests, is intended for readers to share with the girls in their lives. With an emphasis on a mother-daughter relationship, the poems cover a wide range of emotions and topics, from shame and depression to self-love and empowerment.

One of the most striking features of this collection is the honesty with which Schifferle writes. The poems are raw and unapologetic, and they offer a glimpse into the author's struggles with mental health and self-esteem.

Another notable aspect of this collection is the way the author speaks directly to her future daughter throughout the book. This creates a sense of intimacy and personal connection between the author and the reader. Schifferle's messages of strength and empowerment are woven throughout the book, with poems like "Outspoken" and "Radical Self-Love" urging readers to embrace their voices and stand up for themselves.

The book also features poems like "If You Inherit My Depression" and "Shame" that speak to the darker side of mental health struggles. These poems are important reminders that it's okay to not be okay and that seeking help is a sign of strength, not weakness.

My Therapist Told Me to Write This: Poems for Our Daughters is a moving and deeply personal collection of poems that offer important messages of self-love, empowerment, and resilience. The book is a valuable resource for readers of all ages, and it serves as a reminder that we are not alone in our struggles.

GABRIELLA PELOSI, LMHC
(CO-FOUNDER OF D&G WELLNESS CONSULTING)

"... a love letter to the past, present and future..."

Jenna peers into the human condition and inside some of the struggles we as women will face throughout our lives — not so much as a warning, but as a beautiful reminder that we are not alone. It is a love letter to the past, present, and future, not just for women and daughters but for all of us on this wild ride.

CRYSTAL BLANKENBAKER, MRES
(MASTER OF RESEARCH IN PSYCHOLOGY)

MY THERAPIST TOLD ME TO WRITE THIS

My Therapist Told Me to Write This

Poems for Our Daughters

JENNA LEE SCHIFFERLE

Tiny Newt Press, LLC

TINY NEWT PRESS
BUFFALO, NY

My Therapist Told Me to Write This
Poems for Our Daughters

Copyright © 2023 by Jenna Lee Schifferle. All rights reserved.
Printed in the United States of America. First edition. For more
information, contact Tiny Newt Press, LLC at
tinynewtpress@gmail.com.

Cover art by Ashley Kirchner.

ISBN 979-8-9869335-0-4

Published by Tiny Newt Press, LLC.
Buffalo, New York.
www.tinynewtpress.org

CONTENTS

DEDICATION

To my mom:

>Thank you for stoking the fire
>that has always burned within me.
>I'm strong because of you.

To my nieces, Riley, Emily, and Evie:

>May you always chase your dreams,
>even when they're messy and
>the world tries to step on them.

READ THIS ONE TOGETHER

I don't have a daughter
yet
But I bet you do
or maybe you have a niece
or a cousin ...
or a friend ...
... or a friend's daughter
Or maybe, like me, you just dream
about a little girl more fearless than you.
Either way, you should read this book with her.

PROLOGUE

Pam looks at me with a stern yet empathetic expression, her short brown bob wise and all knowing. I've just stopped crying, and she has already passed the ceremonial tissues. I fidget with one in my hands, throwing it back and forth in a clump, unused. The leather couch crunches beneath my weight as the silence grows between us.

"I want you to try something," Pam says, waving her pen in the air. "Bear with me."

I roll my eyes in skepticism and exhale from my belly. When she hesitates, I gesture for her to continue.

"Write yourself a letter."

"A letter?"

She nods. "Write yourself a letter from the other side. Pretend you're older and wiser."

"The other side?"

She laughs at my parroting and then sits up straight as a post. Her gaze unnerves me, almost as if she's staring through a microscope at my brain.

"Yes, the other side. The other side of what you're going through."

"And if I don't want to write to myself?"

Pam considers this, leaning her head backward and casting her eyes toward the ceiling. Her pen smacks her notepad as she pendulums it back and forth between her fingers.

"Then write to your future daughter."

TO MY DAUGHTER

S weet Girl,

You don't know me.
I'm not your friend nor your mother (yet),

just a stranger out there in the universe
wishing for everything

for every woman
for every you

starting off or beginning anew.
I'm just here willing these dreams to life,

so you, my dear,
can help them take flight.

SING

Maybe one day
these words will give you wings and
launch you to the skies.

With fresh air to breathe
you'll reclaim your voice
and, oh, how you'll sing!

OUTSPOKEN

You have a voice.
Fragmented
as
it
may
be.
You have a voice.

Even when it's a whisper
you still have it.

Packed with emotion
Flowery? Sometimes sentimental
yet harsh when need be
— Too much so? I disagree. —
You have a voice.

Maybe it's stricken with passion.
Maybe it's lurid with desperation.
Doesn't matter. You still have it.

Fear at the tip of your tongue may threaten it,
conventions may dismiss it,
but it's yours.
You have a voice.

HEARTFELT

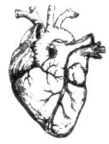

When the world is dark
and tensions thick
close your eyes and listen
to the quiet thumping
of your heart as it
drives your life forward.

Let its constancy
bring you comfort
and remember:
That beat will keep you
going strong.

SHAME

Shame anchors your shoulders
lead
that sinks to soiled toes.
They call you the worst words they can muster
pointed insults floating
in the synapses of your brain —
rewiring, rewiring ...
shame.
Eyes follow you
intense in their condescension
like invisible blades traversing
the distance between you and them
lodging in your memory —
fixating, fixating ...
shame.
What have you done to inherit this monster,
this beast of mankind?
And what will you do now
that he's here to stay?

SHAME: THE RECKONING

"You should be ashamed,"
he'll say.
And you'll smile, exhausted,
because that's one devil
you've already slain.

(I'm proud of you already.)

RAGE

S weet Girl,

    I know why you cry

    out in the middle of the night

                      pleading

    for a hug, a cuddle, a kind word,
    any attention to scare away
    your worst fears
    to convince yourself that you're
    not

                      invisible

    not

                      disappearing

    that you are, in fact,

                      here.

    I know why you cry

    so loud and all-consuming as if it's

                      bursting

    out of your chest and your toes

threatening to

shatter you.

I know why you cry

because I cry, too.
This world has spent
every minute of the last three decades
convincing me that I'm

not enough

that I'm

too much

that tears are weakness
and emotions are savage animals
waiting to be

tamed.

I know why you cry.

You're learning too young.
But please understand this:
Your emotions are

wild, child.

They're meant to be.

Learn their names.
Study them up close.
Figure out how they

prowl

and whom they

protect

and why they

howl.

Then, release your lions
and let them

rage.

RADICAL SELF-LOVE

The hardest thing to do in this life
is to love ourselves
with the fierce, frenzied passion
we deserve
because the world
with its judgments
thinks shame is a gift.
And so we stumble onward
head into the wind
chasing that which eludes us.

IF YOU INHERIT MY DEPRESSION ...

You will have days where you stand beneath an infinite blue sky with rays shining brightly upon your face. Through stiff limbs and a heavy heart, you'll condemn it all, wondering: *What does it mean? What is the point? Why am I here?* Maybe you'll think of ending *it* (substitute *suffering*, substitute *life*). But mostly, you'll just wish you felt alive.

You'll see friends and celebrate their successes while wishing you had purpose — or at least something to toast. You'll raise a glass to their newfound fortune, their path, their happiness, and all the way home, you'll cry at how empty you feel inside. By 9 p.m., you'll be in bed, trying to sleep just to escape your thoughts. This might go on for days or weeks. But most likely, it will last months with varying levels of intensity.

Then one day, you'll have a moment, a fleeting instance, where the sun feels warm and energizing as you shuffle barefoot across the yard with your dog. He'll look back at you, excited to be by your side, sharing this life. Maybe your mom (me!) will chatter excitedly on the phone about her weekend plans, or your fiancé will hug you a little tighter. You'll dig your claws into those moments with everything you've got, as if your life depends upon it — because it does.

Find your moment and don't let go.

TO-DO LIST

When depression hits you again,
you'll pull out all the tricks,
each tip your therapist has given you:

- Find a soft blanket
  run your fingers along it, eyes closed

- Smell a candle
  let the lavender fill your lungs

- Eat a piece of chocolate
  feel guilty but try not to

- Go for a run
  feel the sobs roll through your chest

- Take a shower
  turn up the heat

- Let the hot water burn
  melting away your emotions

- Call your best friend
  realize she's busy

- Call your sister
  realize she hasn't slept since the baby was
  born

- Hang up
  without burdening them

- Try to sleep
  stare at the ceiling for hours

Out of ideas,
you'll fish for one last tool:

- Write to your daughter

  Sweet Girl,
  you're not alone.

READ THIS FIRST

I hope to one day read your notes
on postcards, boasting
about the places you've been
and the adventures you've had.

I hope to one day read your stories
on parchment, painting
a picture of the joy in your heart
and the infinite feeling in your soul.

I hope to one day read your memories
in your memoir, shaping
a narrative and framing it
however you damn well please.

I hope to one day read the happiness
in your laugh lines, decorating
your corner of the universe and
my whole world.

I hope to never read your note
on finely lined paper, revealing
fissures in your façade and
cracks in your confidence.

I hope to never read your desperation
in a letter, asking
for forgiveness, for understanding
after the fact, after goodbye.

I hope you one day hear these words
in my voice, whispering
that you're not alone
and never will be.

I hope you one day read this first.

TO THE WOMAN YOU'LL BE

Confident
Energized
Eager
Strong and
Unstoppable
with shoulders that prop up the world

~~Maybe~~ one day, you'll be her
You'll be her and — wow —
will you dazzle

Sugar and spice,
ready to roll the dice

But today, if you sit
with sadness

Sheepish
Tired
Hesitant
Struggling and

Stuck
with shoulders that sag beneath the load

It's okay

~~Maybe~~ one day, you'll leave her
You'll leave Sadness behind and — wow —
will you dazzle

PROUD

We stand on the shoulders of giants
Women with strong arms and bold, fearless hearts
Women who've faced lifetimes of adversity
yet overcome, overcome, overcome
They blaze trails, smash ceilings, lead the way
so that we can rise ever more
Sisters, daughters, you and me
here to write history
The question remains:
What greatness shall we achieve?
How can we make them proud
all the days of our lives?

CRAVING: A STORY
OF A GIRL

Behind stage at practice ...
At the back of the school bus ...
In a secluded spot of the library ...
On the shower floor ...

This is a tribute to a girl
who needed *it*.

Food, of course —
get your head out of the gutter.

She wouldn't let a calorie pass her lips
lest the gnawing hunger
trick her into growing.

And so she danced with dizziness,
hit the ground hard
(not running)

Passing out was easier
than facing the mirror.

Sweet Girl,
Don't be ~~me~~ her.

IF YOU'RE FEELING

Baby, if you're sad and don't know why,
let yourself feel down.
Sometimes your sadness just needs someone
to hold it, hear it, help it heal
and then
release it.

Baby, if you're heavy and feeling blue
use it to paint the skies
so you can soar beyond these walls,
land on softer grounds
and then
drift higher.

Baby, if you're bored and feeling uninspired
look past the now and toward the hills.
In the background, miracles
roll for miles and wonders
careen down their steep
slopes.

Baby, if all you do is make it through,
I'm still so proud of you.

ACCEPTED

Your soul shakes
                    with
                                        power
                    with
                                        strength
                    too
                                        fierce
                    for form

                    too
                                        valuable
                    for solid ground

                    Let them
wrangle
                    with their
misconceptions
                    and
misjudge
                    you

You were meant for

wide open skies

and

never

touching

down

And when you learn to

fly

the world will

shift

before you
and make the whole

universe

your home

THE LOVE THAT HURTS
AND THE LOVE THAT HEALS

AGE 16, chasing each other around the school
falling back against the soft grass
with beads of sweat slithering down your face.

You look over and catch his eyes —
soft, blue
infinite as a cloudless sky.

Your stomach hurts from belly laughing
at inside jokes
and your skin burns
on fire where his shoulder brushes yours.

You can't imagine
can't fathom
life without ...
a future where
you aren't his
(He's not yours.)

Nevertheless, when you meet *the one* years later
(*the one* he'll call *everything*)
you'll smile
as the little girl inside you
falls apart.

AGE 29, dancing around the kitchen
the radio singing a jazzy note
as beads of sweat drip down your wine glass.

You look up and he's staring at you
eyes bright brown
reassuring as a warm embrace.

Your stomach hurts from belly laughing
at how young you feel
and your heart overflows
as his lips brush yours

You can't imagine,
can't fathom
life without ...
a future where
you aren't his
(He is yours.)

Nevertheless, when you meet him at the altar years later
(*the one* you'll call *husband*)
you'll smile as the woman inside you
falls more in love.

SHE/ HE/ THEY

S weet Girl,

If ever there's a day
where you say to yourself
I love her
Don't come to me to confess.

Invite her to dinner
and hold her hand
and know that I'll love her
just as I love you.

S weet Girl,

If ever there's a day
where you say to yourself
I am him
Don't come to me to confess.

Tell me once what you prefer
and hold my hand
knowing that I'll love you
as him, as her, as they.

My sweet child

GROW

S weet Child,

> You won't always know better
> You'll act from inexperience,
> false assumptions
> and a dash of
> vanity
>
> Your gut won't always lunge
> when something's not right
> You'll be blissful in
> unawareness
>
> You won't realize your impact
> or how you affect others
> but you will
> learn
>
> So will those who've wronged you
> Once they learn better —
> forgive

Once you learn better —
do better

This is the only way to
change the world

FALL FORWARD

Darling,

Don't live for perfection
Don't let the weight of failure stop you
from moving forward
You may trip
                                                                                                                       &
        fall
but when you stand back up
you'll be
a   foot   in   the   right   direction
Don't play it
                      safe
Don't stay in your
                      lane
Learn the joy of   c
                 r   o
           e   m
       v   i
     o   n
                      g

The view from the top is sweeter
when you've

                              hit
                              rock
                              bottom

and discovered
how

                    rise

          can

     you
high

                         So fall,

                         baby,

                         fall

          Then lift yourself up by the teeth and
          take a bite out of the mountain before you.

MY THERAPIST TOLD ME TO WRITE THIS

Don't fret, child.
It's just a phase,
struggling to get by
in this day and age.

Stop those tears, child.
You need time to mend.
Your true friends will be there
in the end.

Try to smile, child,
when it hurts you so.
Trials are there
to help you grow.

Focus, child,
on your dreams and your heart.
Out of pain
comes the finest art.

You aren't perfect, child.

Don't aim to be.
Just try your best
and let it be.

You need to stand
on your own two feet
and not rely
on everyone you meet.

There are people, child,
who will let you down.
That's not an excuse
for your heavy frown.

Child, learn to let it go.
This is the only way
you'll ever
grow

Now close your eyes
and rest a while.
Everything will be okay
for you, my child.

EPILOGUE

S weet Child,

Today while reading my notebook
a thought struck me straight
over the head.

>If I'd let my
>emotions win,
>given in to the sorrow,
>I'd never have the pleasure
>of getting to know you
>or being your mother —
>and that just won't do.

Jenna Lee
Schifferle

J enna wrote *My Therapist Told Me to Write This* over the course of several years as a way of working through her own struggles with mental health. Though she doesn't have a daughter, she hopes her words will help someone's child feel less alone.

A portion of the proceeds from every book sold will benefit the Mental Health Advocates of Western New York.

Jenna holds a Bachelor's degree in journalism and creative writing from SUNY Oswego and a Master's degree in English literature from the University of Rochester. Her work has appeared in *Aurora Poetry*, *In Good Health—Buffalo*, *The Lockport Union-Sun & Journal*, *Syracuse Woman Magazine*, *The Oswegonian*, *Blink-Ink,* and *Chicken Soup for the Soul: Curvy and Confident.* Two of her stories were also honored with a Syracuse Press Club Award and New York Press Association Award. *My Therapist Told Me to Write This* is her first collection of poetry.

Jenna lives in Buffalo, New York, with her husband and pets.

Website: www.jennaschifferle.wordpress.com
Instagram: @jenna_lee_writes

www.ingramcontent.com/pod-product-compliance
Lightning Source LLC
Chambersburg PA
CBHW060255150626
46553CB00019BA/2370